THE
GRETA
THUNBERG
STORY

BEING DIFFERENT IS A SUPERPOWER

MICHAEL PART

Sole BOOKS

To Craig Meyer, Los Angeles Pierce College

Proof: Louisa Jordan
Cover design: Nick Part, Lazar Kackarovski
Layout: Lazar Kackarovski
Cover photo: AP Photo/Kirsty Wiggleswort

ISBN: 978-1-938591-74-7
E-Book ISBN: 978-1-938591-75-4

Library of Congress Cataloging-in-Publication data available.

Printed in the United States of America.

Published by Sole Books. First edition: September 2019

www.solebooks.com

"I was fortunate to be born in a time and place where everyone told us to dream big; I could become whatever I wanted to. I could live wherever I wanted to. People like me had everything we needed and more. Things our grandparents could not even dream of. We had everything we could ever wish for and yet now we may have nothing. Now we probably don't even have a future anymore."

~ Greta Thunberg ~
April 23, 2019

TABLE OF CONTENTS

CHAPTER ONE

NO SCHOOL TODAY

At precisely 8:30 in the morning of Monday, August 20, 2018, a young girl of 15 with Pippi Longstocking pigtails arrived by bicycle at the Stockholm Parliament. The weather was nice and the ride from home was a breeze. She got off her bike and found a spot where she could sit in front of the passageway to the building and be noticed by as many passersby as possible.

Greta Thunberg plunked down next to her wooden sign painted white with bold black lettering on the warm concrete leading to the imposing Parliament building overlooking the river and leaned back against the bricks. The sign said: *School Strike for Climate*.

She sat there holding the sign, her heart pounding. She wondered what it would be like sitting here for the next three weeks. The sun shone bright and the first hour passed as if everything was ordinary and normal. Hundreds of people passed by and some smiled at her, but mostly, no one stopped. She checked her watch. Her plan was to stay here from 8:30 in the morning until 3:30 in the afternoon.

A shadow fell across her face and she looked up. It was a Member of Parliament. He crossed his arms in a scolding fashion and looked down at her with bright blue eyes. "Why aren't you in school?" he asked.

Greta grinned politely. "What's the point?"

The MP stiffened. "What do you mean, what's the point? The point is to learn!"

Greta gave him a stern look. "My teacher stopped showing up."

The MP raised an eyebrow. "Surely the school will have already found a substitute teacher," he said and looked around. A small crowd gathered. "I don't see any other of your fellow students."

"No, I am the only one," Greta replied. "So far."

"That's absurd, why wouldn't your teacher show up?"

"She had something better to do," Greta replied. "I believe she went to New York."

The MP, obviously frustrated, changed the subject by studying her wooden sign. "I do not understand this strike of yours."

Greta was ready. She spoke calmly. "I am striking for the climate. Earth is in mortal danger and nothing is being done about it. Unless we do something, until Sweden is in line with the Paris Agreement, everything is meaningless and there is no future for me, so what is the point of going to school?"

The MP studied Greta. "What makes you think we aren't doing anything about climate change?"

Greta cocked her head, a move she learned from Moses, her Golden Retriever. "I don't have to think about it, we are not aligned with the Paris Agreement. In fact, Sweden is tenth in the world. We might as well be last, if we are not first."

This irritated the MP. "Is this what they teach you in school?"

"No, I learned this all on my own," Greta replied. "No teacher, remember?"

"Do your parents know you are out here?"

"Of course," Greta replied.

"Don't they think you should be in school?"

"Of course," Greta said. "But they also know why I am doing this. As parents, they think it's bad."

"There you go!" the MP exclaimed.

"But as fellow human beings," Greta said, "they think it's good."

The MP scowled. He didn't expect that answer. "You think you're pretty smart, don't you?"

Greta shrugged. "Average."

The days in Sweden were long in August. The sun rose at around 4:30 am and did not set until a little after 9 pm at night. This was because Stockholm Sweden's absolute location on Earth was 59.3293 degrees North and 18.0686 degrees East. Sweden is quite a bit north of most things and if you drew a straight line from it across the North Atlantic, it would cut right through the Labrador Sea before it finally smacked into Canada, somewhere in

Newfoundland where the Inuit, an indigenous people of Northern Canada who hunt and fish, discovered their ice was melting.

Greta made those kinds of calculations frequently as it was of utmost importance that she know exactly where she was on the planet at any given moment. Although most people thought it strange, there was actually nothing odd about it.

Some birds sang nearby and although Greta played the piano, she could not identify which keys they were in. That was her mother's job. She was an opera singer.

Those kinds of sounds, those that didn't go together, hurt Greta's ears. There were many sounds that made her wince and cover her ears because besides having Asperger's on the autism spectrum, she also had a fun feature known as misophonia, and this superpower affected her emotionally. People chewing, for instance, drove her nuts.

By 3:30 in the afternoon, Greta had had exactly zero visitors other than the MP and although many people marched by on their way to work and shopping in the city, exactly zero people asked her exactly zero questions.

She rode her bike for twenty minutes to her home and exactly zero people asked her about her painted wooden sign. She planned to strike until election day on September 9. Nineteen days to go—and she wasn't ready to give up.

On the second day, Greta sat on a camping mat in front of the rose-colored Parliament. Hundreds of people walked by, but no one stopped for hours. Then, the same MP stopped and watched Greta but said nothing. After four or five minutes of awkward silence, a man and a woman squatted down on either side of her. The MP looked from one of the new arrivals to the other. "Don't tell me you're joining this little girl," he said. "Aren't you a little too old for school?"

The man smiled and nodded. "Perhaps too old for school, but not too old to strike," he said and nodded his head toward Greta and they laughed. Greta remained quiet. "Why don't you join us?"

The MP rolled his eyes and snorted in frustration. He walked off, straightening his tie and shoving his umbrella under his arm. "The kids these days!" he muttered to himself as he took one last backward glance at Greta and the newly-arrived couple, then charged up the stairs to Parliament.

Greta looked at the man sitting to her right, and the woman sitting to her left, and smiled. "I don't think he understands that school works better when the teachers show up."

"How long you been doing this?" the man asked.

"This is my second day. But I'm going to be here every day until two days before the election on September 9. Morning till afternoon. How about you? You here for climate change?"

The man smiled and blushed. "Actually, we're here for you. We're reporters."

"Oh?"

"So, Greta Thunberg, why are you on strike?"

Greta was surprised. "You know my name?" She knitted her brows to let them know she was suspicious.

"We asked around," the man said. "You're the daughter of the singer Malena Ernman and actor Svante Thunberg."

Greta just stared at them.

"Your parents approve of this, I suppose," the woman said.

Greta nodded. She was bored.

"Now you're here, striking for the climate," the man said. "Why?"

"It started with an island," Greta said.

"An island?"

"Yes. In 2014. That island changed everything."

"Where is this island?" the woman asked.

"Off the coast of Chile."

"Oh!" the woman exclaimed. "You mean Easter Island?"

"No," Greta said. "This island has no name and is made entirely of garbage. And it is as big as the country of Mexico!"

The reporters looked at each other then turned to Greta. "Okay, you have our attention."

Greta took a deep breath. Speaking to people outside of her immediate family was new to her. It was all part of the change in her life. She spoke clearly and precisely, in black and white, telling them all about it.

CHAPTER TWO

TRAVELS

Greta loved to travel and, being the daughter of an opera singer, she was fortunate to have seen the great places of Europe, most of which she remembered in great detail.

The first time she remembered travel was the following year, in 2007, when they all went to Vienna, in Austria. She remembered Vienna because there was so much detail attached to all the old buildings: gargoyles and statues were everywhere in rich relief and so far up off the ground, it was hard to see them from the street. Her mother played Sesto in *Giulio Cesare* by George Frideric Handel.

Although Greta was intrigued by the complicated architecture of the city of Vienna, she loved the hotel room where they stayed. It had no kitchen and no cooking was allowed, her mother explained, when Greta asked about the oven she could not find. Curiously, for the four-year-old, men and woman appeared out of nowhere with carts of steaming food and chocolates they hid under the pillows when they turned down the beds. Beata, her younger sister, was just one year old and followed Greta everywhere and frequently made a lot of noise.

Even then, during their travels all over Europe, her mother and father made sure their girls understood about conserving water by not wasting it on too many baths, even though they were fun, and also the importance of eating all their food. "Do not take more than you can eat," Malena scolded Greta. "We must be environmentally conscious, not waste water, and not waste food either. In fact, your father's relative from a long time ago was a pioneer in the environment and we must live up to the work he did."

Greta wondered who she meant.

One cold evening, when the Thunbergs were back in their home in Stockholm, Malena showed the children how to conserve energy by closing the windows when she heated the room. Outside, across the cityscape, Greta watched the chimneys of all the homes and buildings and factories, far and wide, belching smoke.

"Is smoke dirty, Mom?" Greta asked.

"Of course, it is," Malena replied.

"Then why does everybody do it?"

"Not everybody," Malena said. "Not us." She smiled.

It was not long after that, when Greta was five, that she first saw the small row of old books written by a man named Svante Arrhenius way up high on the shelf next to her mother's music books; high enough where she could never reach them. "He was my great-grandmother's cousin," her dad said. "I was named after him."

Seven years later, in 2014, when she was 11 years old, after studying and marveling at the family bookshelf for more than an hour, Greta stretched her hand up and took down the blue book entitled *Worlds in the Making* by Svante Arrhenius, published in 1908. The book was about how Earth captured some of the outpouring of energy and heat from the sun. She had had her eye on it over the years because she liked the title and one day it was hers because she could finally reach it. Arrhenius was fascinating. He was a student of the climatologist John Tyndall and a college professor and she was astounded to discover he had won the Nobel Prize for Chemistry in 1903.

Malena found Greta curled up in a corner of the room next to the bookcase, reading the little blue book.

"He also discovered the Greenhouse Effect," Malena said. "Took him a year. Drove him crazy, so the story goes."

Greta looked up from the book. "The Greenhouse Effect?" She smiled. "I like the sounds of those words." She wrinkled her nose. "What is it?"

Malena came closer. "It is what happens when there is too much carbon dioxide in the air. Our atmosphere traps it, keeps it locked in, and the planet heats up. Like a hothouse. Nowadays, the scientists call it *climate change*. It is why your father and I always insist we conserve water and food and electricity and never allow smoke to bellow from our chimney.

Greta's eyes widened as her mother spoke.

"The whole world is in a crisis that we humans created through our lifestyle," she said. "We became too detached from nature. We need to find our way back. Doing the things we have practiced as a family all these years is all right, but we are just one family."

"At least we are doing something," Greta chimed in.

"Yes, it is a crisis that affects us all and could destroy the planet if we don't change the way we live and behave."

"But we already did change, Mom," Greta said. "We do those things."

"We need everybody to do it," Malena replied.

Greta and Beata had heard these words their whole life and now they were connected to the name on the book who discovered it.

"Mom, if humans could really change the climate, everybody would be talking about it all the time. And they're not. They're talking about everything else."

Malena smiled at her daughter. She was a handful, but nothing escaped her sharp mind, even at her age. "Yes, but like I said, it starts with us, darling," she said.

"Even me?" Greta asked.

"Of course," Malena replied. "Even you." She held out her hand and Greta took it and she pulled her daughter to her feet. "But how do you expect to save the planet if you don't get any sleep?"

"But I'm not tired," Greta complained.

Malena smiled. "You can take the book with you."

Greta smiled and picked up the little blue book and allowed her mother to guide her to bed.

CHAPTER THREE

SHUTTING DOWN

A few hours later, the aria "Habanera" filled the room with music. It was from the opera *Carmen* by the French composer, Georges Bizet, and when Greta's mother's voice came in, singing in French, *"L'amour est un oiseau rebelle,"* which meant "Love is a rebellious bird," Greta's heart leaped. She knew what the words meant as she'd heard her mother rehearse it hundreds of times and it gave her chills every time she sang it. Malena Ernman's mezzo-soprano voice was perfect and reminded Greta of the birds outside their window most mornings. Malena leaned against the wall next to a picture of her two daughters, arms crossed, eyes closed. It was a lot of work putting out this album and she was glad it was finished.

"Magnificent!" Svante said and took his wife's hand. "Your finest album yet!"

The cover lay on the floor, its title showing: *Opera di Fiori*

"You know," Svante cooed, "'*Carmen* is my favorite of yours."

"Yes," Malena said with a wink. "And I know why." She twirled into his arms. He was a bit taller than she and Greta thought they looked perfect together.

"Which is *your* favorite?" Svante asked.

Malena chuckled with a twinkle in her eye. "You know as well as I that my favorite is always the next one," she replied. "*Xerxes*."

Svante grinned. "It had better be. We have a lot of money riding on it, producing it ourselves. I have no doubt, the Archipelag will ring out when you bring your voice to it again!" The Archipelag was the opera house near the ocean in Stockholm and her favorite.

Malena blushed. "Being close to the sea air does wonders for my coloratura. So they say." She blushed, realizing she was bragging. It embarrassed her.

Malena was a mezzo-soprano, a soprano who could also sing contralto, and the coloratura was what she added musically to her performance, like adding an ornament to a Christmas tree.

Svante held her. "It will be your finest performance."

She managed a smile. "Also, my last," she said. She was going to retire. They had discussed it. She wanted to devote more time to raising her girls.

Beata beamed and Malena noticed. "Why are *you* so happy?"

"Because *you* won't always be gone so much," she said.

Malena hugged her. "You're right. I need to be around all of you more. You *do* need me, don't you?" she kidded.

"Yes!" Beata shouted and hugged her again.

Greta smiled, but the whole idea of retiring worried her. They had discussed it over and over, especially every time she stopped talking or Beata threw a fit, but she also knew she was being selfish. For Greta, no more operas meant no more traveling, something she loved with all her heart. Then something caught the corner of her eye. Although they were all in the living room, the light was still on in the kitchen. "Mother, be a dear and turn out the kitchen light," she quipped. "Conservation."

Malena realized her daughter had just turned the tables on her and laughed uproariously.

It was a laugh that was pure music and happiness to Greta's ears and she never forgot it because it would be a long time before she would be able to capture those feelings of happiness again.

The next morning, she went to school as usual, but the teacher did something unusual: he showed a documentary on the condition of the world and its fragile environment.

Greta watched the film and as pictures of starving polar bears set to music bombarded her senses, weather events like floods and hurricanes and tornadoes destroyed villages, all ending with the discovery of an island off the coast of Chile made entirely of plastic garbage—as big as the country of Mexico—it was too much for her.

She grew sad. Worried. She felt like everything was slipping away and where she thought her life had meaning, it suddenly did not. She drifted into depression. No one in the classroom noticed but Greta. Not even the teacher, who continued lecturing as if a gigantic island made of garbage was normal.

"Greta, your mother is not only a well-known opera singer, she is also very well known for her work with conservation, I've spoken with her. Your family has a lot of experience with the environment. Perhaps you would like to share your feelings about the film."

"I am beyond upset," Greta forced out of her lips. She didn't want to say anything else. Something was happening inside her.

"Oh," the teacher said, surprised.

"I should be," Greta continued. "This is terrible. I am worried sick. Our planet is in peril. What are we doing about it?"

The teacher shrugged. "We can only hope someone does something about it," she said. "Climate Science is a real thing, but not everybody believes in it."

Greta was mortified. "Why? How could that be? Don't they believe their own eyes? Don't they believe in science?"

Some of the students in class began to laugh at her.

Greta could feel the tears welling-up in her eyes. She grew even sadder. "Science is science," she muttered. "Isn't it?" She felt herself shutting down.

It was as if everything she was taught, everything she believed in, was just proven wrong.

The teacher was as frustrated as Greta. "It is," she said. "But unfortunately, it's bad for business. The oil industry, for example. They fight against the science because their business depends on it."

Greta studied her. *Why is she telling us this*? She didn't want to know that it was worse than she thought. She shook her head, angry and frustrated. She didn't want to say another word. It was all too much for her. She burst out crying. The entire classroom erupted in laughter. The teacher didn't know what to do.

"I–I will not be here on Monday," she said. "I am going to a wedding in New York."

Greta stared at her in disbelief. The starving polar bears, the island of garbage, the dying earth, all a footnote. The lunch bell rang and the students all raced out of class. Greta went last and took another look at her teacher, her back to her, erasing the blackboard. A short while later, Greta stood in line in the cafeteria with her usual tray, but when the food server tried to give her a hamburger, she refused it. "But you always eat this, Greta," the woman said.

Greta looked at the burger. "I can't. It's the ground-up meat of a living thing!" She raced out of the cafeteria without eating and when she got outside, began to cry again.

Greta was not herself when she got home. Malena noticed first and asked her what was wrong, but Greta did not answer. She ignored her parents and her sister and went to sit next to Moses, the family's Golden Retriever. She stroked his fur. Minutes turned to hours. Both Malena and Svante tried to talk to her but she refused to speak. She eventually stopped crying, but her actions were upsetting to the whole family. They desperately wanted to know what was going on.

But Greta's lips were sealed. She refused to speak and refused to eat, even a single bite. It grew late and eventually Greta was sent to bed where she shut the bedroom door and cried in bed for hours.

In the morning, Svante drove her to school. He tried to talk to her but she remained mute.

She didn't talk in school. She didn't eat. The teacher eventually called him. He got in the car, drove to school, and brought her back home to Moses.

Again, she refused to eat and didn't say a word.

No-one knew why.

As far as Greta was concerned, her lips were sealed, by worry and depression. And she would not allow anything to pry them open again.

She was shutting down. Like turning off the ignition of a gas-guzzling car, and throwing away the key.

To Svante and Malena, days turned to weeks as they tried to coax her to eat and to speak;

they knew something was seriously wrong with their oldest daughter and they were bound and determined to find out what it was. Malena indeed, stopped performing after her final performance of *Xerxes* and vowed to dedicate all her time to her daughters, particularly Greta, who would barely eat and refused to speak except when absolutely necessary.

CHAPTER FOUR

ASPERGER'S & AVOCADOS

Malena cooked gnocchi. The Italian dumplings were always one of Greta's favorite dishes.

Yet she refused to eat them.

She offered her avocados, another favorite.

Again, Greta refused them. She refused everything.

Malena wanted to cry but held back her tears. She had to stay strong. In desperation, willing to try anything, she devised a plan to make the whole eating thing more interesting and yet at the same time, nourishing. Greta's health was at serious risk and Malena and Svante could not bear seeing their daughter suffer.

Malena went to the stove and brought the pot of gnocchi over to her. "What's wrong with the gnocchi?" she asked.

"Too sticky," Greta replied, staring at the table, not wanting to meet her mother's eyes.

Malena handed the pot back to Svante. "Please cook them a little more," she said to him, and Svante put the pot back on the burner and cooked them for another minute. Then, Malena took one from the pot and placed it on Greta's plate, blowing on it to cool it off. "See how that is."

Greta looked at her father, then her mother, then picked the gnocchi up and smelled it, rolled it around in her hand and set it back down, nodding.

"All right," Malena said. "Let's eat ten of them."

"That's the wrong number," Greta said, shaking her head.

Malena sighed. "What is the correct number?"

Greta thought about it. "Three."

Malena shook her head. "Three is not enough to nourish you. It's not healthy."

Greta remained silent.

"Seven," Malena said. "Seven bites. That's not too much to ask."

Greta shook her head. "Five."

Malena looked askance at her husband, then returned her gaze to her most difficult negotiating partner. "All right. Five." She nodded to her husband who spooned five gnocchi onto Greta's plate. Malena smiled.

Greta smiled back, then turned her attention to the five gnocchi on her plate. She stared at them for twenty minutes.

Malena and Svante felt as if they were growing old right in front of her. Finally, after twenty minutes, Greta picked up one gnocchi with her fork and turned it around in front of her face, sniffed it, then nibbled off a bite so tiny it would be considered transparent. She chewed. Swallowed. Then bit off another chunk and ate it. Nineteen minutes later, she finished the first gnocchi.

Two hours and ten minutes later, she finished the last gnocchi. "I'm full," she said. "I cannot eat anymore."

Malena slumped in her chair and Svante, standing near the stove, blew out a breath of relief.

A few weeks later, they tried making cinnamon buns. Greta sniffed them, didn't like, could not fit them in her mouth, and freaked out and cried for over an hour with an anxiety attack. Moses snuggled up to her and calmed her down.

Two long months passed. Greta had lost over ten pounds from not eating. For Malena and Svante, it was a nightmare; a long, perilous journey to get to the bottom of what had made Greta shut down with no definite answer. Fearing for their daughter's life, they finally took her to the Astrid Lindgren Children's Hospital and the Stockholm Center for Eating Disorders.

As the family drove to the Stockholm Center, Greta watched out the window in the backseat. Beata usually sat next to her in back, but she was still in school and her grandmother Mona, her father's mother, would pick her up, so Greta was alone in back.

"Will I be well again?" she asked, looking out the window. The leaves had turned to shades of yellow and orange and golden brown. It was already fall in Sweden. For Greta, however, there were no seasons. Only despair.

"Of course, you will be well again," Malena said, turning around in the front seat to face her.

Greta studied her mother for an eternity. "When?"

Malena glanced at Svante, who was driving, then shook her head. "I don't know."

Before leaving for the Center, Greta had selected a book to read while they waited for the tests and the results.

"Which book did you choose, Greta?" Svante asked as they navigated the streets of Stockholm to the Center.

"Your great-grandmother's cousin's book," she said with a grin. "The blue one."

Svante chuckled and looked over at his wife sitting next to him.

An hour later, after Greta had gone through a handful of grueling tests, a psychiatrist finally stuck his head into the waiting room.

Greta looked up first. She already knew the answer. She had done her own research over the past few months. She knew what she had and it wasn't that eating disorder, anorexia.

That was a treacherous disease that hid itself. Greta stopped eating for a reason. She was worried sick about Earth.

"Asperger's syndrome," the psychologist said when she got the family alone in a room. "Also, it is quite clear that she is on the autism spectrum."

Malena burst out crying.

"It's a bit complicated to explain, but it doesn't have to be a handicap for Greta. She is rigid in her thinking, yes. Obsessive. A perfectionist. There is generally a right way to do things and to her, it merely means if someone does it differently, she may get confused. Everything is in black and white in her mind."

Greta gasped.

"What's wrong?" Malena asked, comforting her daughter.

"She's right! Except for the autism part. I looked it up."

The psychologist grinned. "Oh?" The psychologist said. "But if you looked it up you must already know that Asperger's isn't technically a diagnosis by itself. It is always part of a broader category called ASD—Autism Spectrum Disorder. In how many places did you look to come to that conclusion?"

Greta blanched. "Why, one of course."

The psychologist grinned. "Of course. You would only want to refer to one. Because of the Asperger's."

Greta laughed. "You're right again!"

Malena recognized it as her "key of C" laugh because most things she heard were in terms of musical notes.

It was a musical laugh and she covered her mouth with her hands to stop it, as she was surprised at her own outburst. "Of course, she is right, Greta."

"Thank you," said the psychologist.

Svante gave Malena a handkerchief and she dabbed her eyes. "But what about her eating?" she sobbed. "Her depression? Just because we know the diagnosis, doesn't change anything for Greta, does it?"

"If there is no change by the weekend, we'll have to admit her to the hospital for treatment," the psychologist said.

Greta suddenly looked worried. "But—I don't need a hospital," she said.

"I'm afraid, if you are starving, there is no other way."

Greta remained quiet, the wheels in her head turning.

A few minutes later, the appointment over, Greta and her family left by the private rear staircase to the street. Greta did not want to use the elevator.

Greta went first down the stairs and seemed happier. She always went first, and when she reached the bottom step, she turned back to face her mother and father. "I want to start eating again," she said.

This time it was Malena's turn to gasp.

"When we get home, we can try a banana," Svante said.

"No," Greta said. "I want to eat normally again. Asperger's and avocados."

Malena chuckled.

Svante, who was an actor by profession, was usually never at a loss for words. Except this time. His mood changed instantly. He was happy again. Tears welled-up in his eyes. He hadn't cried this whole time, despite all the stress of dealing with Greta's condition. He let go. Tears streamed down his cheeks and he usually hid them but this time he didn't care. This caused Malena to join in the crying and that caused Greta to join in as well. Within seconds, all three were crying their eyes out in the car, and cried most of the way home.

When Greta came into their home, Moses greeted them and she hugged him tight. "Moses knows I'm going to be all right," she said.

CHAPTER FIVE

TO LIVE LIKE A REFUGEE

After months of not eating, Greta woke up with hope and the veil of her deep depression fell away like the shedding of an old skin. The minute she got home from the clinic, she ate a whole green apple, then decided on a diet that she never wanted to change: rice, avocados, bananas, calcium tablets, and pancakes. She loved to stuff pancakes with rice. Because she had Asperger's, she never varied. It was the oneness of Asperger's.

The next morning, she knew what she had to do and began making plans in her head, where it was safe, until she could work out the details.

Christmas rolled around and Greta had problems at school again. The previous fall, Beata had entered the 4th Grade and Greta entered the 7th. Her depression melted away under the therapy of Sertraline, an antidepressant also known as Zoloft. With her symptoms in check, Greta's intelligence blossomed. She regained her photographic memory and, among other things, could recite the entire Periodic Table of Elements in less than a minute.

Although Greta's teachers were impressed with her intelligence and scholarship, a number of her fellow students were not. Greta rarely spoke to anyone; it was just not her. The other students did not understand when she didn't answer back when they greeted her. Instead of understanding her autism and Asperger's, they thought she thought she was better than them. A few of them decided to do something about it. And one day when she stepped out of the restroom, a trio of girls jumped her and beat her up.

She walked home with cuts and bruises on her face and arms and a black eye. When she got home, Malena and Beata treated her cuts and iced her black eye.

Svante came in and kissed his daughter's forehead. "Don't worry, little one, we'll handle this."

"Oh?" Malena snapped. She had had it with all of this. "What are we going to do?"

Greta smiled. "Mom, all Swedes know the best place to find a helping hand is at the end of your own arm," she said, reciting an old Swedish Proverb.

Malena burst out laughing. "You are absolutely right, Greta!"

The next day—Malena and Svante—worried and angry, showed up at school.

The superintendent smiled at Mr. and Mrs. Thunberg, sitting in identical chairs in front of him. Greta remained outside the office in the waiting room.

"I suppose I should let you know," the superintendent started. "There has been more than one complaint from several students that Greta was behaving strangely."

"My daughter was attacked," Malena snapped. "And you're trying to blame her?!"

"Well I—"

Before he could respond, Svante jumped in. "I'm sure that is not what the superintendent meant, darling," Svante said, turning to the superintendent. "Did you?"

"Well I—" He seemed stuck on that one phrase and could not communicate any further.

"Well, let me help you with your words. What do you mean when you say, 'strangely'?" Svante asked, growing more and more annoyed.

The superintendent opened his clipboard and flipped a page then pointed at a list of things and read them off: "A—a number of children say she speaks too softly when they ask her things or try to talk to her, she uh, never says hello when they greet her," he replied.

Silence fell in the room. Then Malena spoke. "I suppose it's possible you are the last to know, but I find it hard to believe," she spat, growing louder with every word.

"I—I'm sorry, I don't understand. Last to know what?" The superintendent grew nervous.

"Greta is on the spectrum. Asperger's." She had lost all patience and Svante glanced over and motioned her to calm down with his eyes.

"I—I wasn't aware of—" He didn't finish his sentence.

Svante and Malena exchanged looks. They knew they had to find another school. They had to protect their daughter.

A week later, before Greta returned to school with a new plan, she leaned forward in her chair in the living room, her eyes glued to the television set. She watched the news. And it was horrible. The war in Syria was taking a toll and millions of migrants were fleeing across the war-torn desert and over the Mediterranean Sea to Europe.

"Beata, come quick!" she called and Beata came in from her room and sat down next to her older sister and watched. "This is terrible," she said. "We must do something."

"But we're just kids," Beata said. "Especially me."

Greta thought about it. "It doesn't matter, there must be something we can do to help," she said.

The city of Stockholm is situated on fourteen islands, on the banks of the Stockholm archipelago where Lake Märlaren meets the Baltic Sea. There are numerous other islands in Stockholm county and the sixteenth largest island in the area is Ingarö and is riddled with petroglyphs, evidence of it being inhabited since the Nordic Bronze Age. For most in Sweden, Ingarö is a treat; for Greta's family, it is paradise. They built a summer home there to be near where Malena performed her operas in the Archipelag, 33 kilometers from the center of Stockholm.

One important fact about the Swedes: they are committed to helping people in need. Rejecting injustice is in their bloodstreams. The Thunbergs were no exception.

In the fall of 2015, Ingarö became more than a summer home for Greta and her family when the migrant crisis struck Europe. Millions of migrants came by land and sea from Kosovo, Afghanistan, Albania, Iraq, and many other countries. Most of the migrants came from Syria as it grew more and more dangerous in the war that ravaged its landscape. Many Syrians wound up in Germany and from there migrated up to Norway and Sweden, looking for someplace to live.

Greta wrung her hands nervously. "They need a place to live. They're all homeless," she said.

"What can we do?" Beata asked.

Greta thought about it. "Let them live in our summer house on Ingarö!"

"All of them?!" Beata exclaimed.

Greta smiled. "That would be a sight, wouldn't it? They would fill up the house and all the other houses on the island and all the fields and roads and the ocean all the way back to Stockholm!"

Beata blushed. "You're right. Let's start with one family."

"Good idea," Greta replied.

CHAPTER SIX

OPEN HEARTS

Svante and Malena stood in the walkway of their summer home on Ingarö Island and Beata and Greta stood in front of them. Greta was anxious and shifted from one foot to the other, waiting. Beata stared down at the concrete walkway, making sure her left foot was forward, always in the right spot on the cement square.

"There they are!" Greta exclaimed. "Our Syrian guests!"

The bus pulled to a stop at the edge of the Thunberg property and the front door whispered open and the family exited. The man turned and waved to the driver, who waved back and closed the door and the bus roared away up the road that was a loop around the small island.

The Thunbergs had paid for the bus, just as they had paid for the living materials and food for the family until they reached the island home. Mother and father carried suitcases and their three children, all younger than Greta and Beata, had state-provided backpacks, bulging with new clothing, and fruits and crackers and nuts to munch on their long journey from Germany to Stockholm by train and finally to Ingarö Island.

The guests looked around in wonder as they walked toward the home. The children were silent and glum. Their journey began long before they reached Sweden and Gotland Island, which was where all refugees were brought first after a long and arduous journey that began with a hundred-mile march in the worn-out shoes of a casualty who no longer needed them and ended on a bus at the Thunberg doorstep.

"My God," Malena muttered under her breath to her husband, shocked at the realization that this was no ordinary family, but the survivors of a terrible war not far enough away from Sweden to not be felt.

The father stepped forward and greeted his newly-adopted family and both families went inside to get to know each other.

Over the months of fall and winter, the Thunbergs visited their guests on weekends. The family spun tales of Damascus and what happened in war-torn Syria, and cooked their favorite dishes. Greta bent over the stove and tables and smelled the stews and dishes, but never touched the food when it came to eating. Beata, on the other hand, bravely ate her way through all of the Syrian cuisine.

Greta was polite, but stuck to her limited diet that winter. In the spring, Greta and Beata made plans for the new semester.

Winter gave way to spring without fanfare and the Thunbergs were back in their Stockholm home. School started tomorrow and Malena planned Greta's meals and placed them in individual containers so she could bring them to school and keep them in the refrigerator there. She pasted Greta's name tag on each of her lunch containers and stuck them in the refrigerator so the top one would be fresh for tomorrow's lunch.

That evening, while Svante and Malena watched television, Greta disappeared into the kitchen.

Moments later, she screamed bloody murder.

Malena and Svante raced into the kitchen and found Greta frozen in place in front of the refrigerator, holding the door open, shaking her head. "I can't eat it, I can't eat it," she said over and over. "Take it off! Take it off!"

Malena took her daughter in her arms. "Take what off, Greta?" Now *she* was shaking.

"The name tag," she said. "I—I can't eat it if it has my name on it!" She spun out of her mother's arms and raced out of the kitchen and down the hall to her bedroom.

Malena and Svante looked at each other. "I'm never going to get this right," Malena sobbed and fell into her husband's arms.

"Sure, you are," Svante soothed. "Just take her name tag off."

Malena wiped her eyes. "Who knew?" She relaxed and looked into her husband's eyes. "Of course, that would solve everything," she said. "How silly of me." She made it into a joke.

Svante smiled. "We learn something new every day," he said.

"Oh?" Malena said. "And what did we learn today?"

"That raising children is not for wimps."

Malena laughed. "It would have been nice if ours had come with an instruction manual."

Svante laughed while Malena peeled off the name tag and shut the refrigerator. They returned to the living room and their television show.

From that day on, and for a long time after that, Greta only ate what was in that lunch container: pancakes stuffed with rice.

And never with a name tag on it.

CHAPTER SEVEN

THE LIBRARY

B ecause of her fear of being bullied again, the school library became a refuge for Greta. Her teacher taught her secretly two hours a week during recess and gymnastic classes. In those two hours, she made up for her lost time in class. Each day, Greta snuck into the school via the library to avoid the cruelty and bullying from the other students. When school was over, she tiptoed through the library to the outside and to the car, where her dad was waiting for her.

"You can't ignore everyone," Malena said. "You need friends."

Greta shook her head. "I don't need friends. They are just children," she said.

The school had tried to blame Greta for her troubles and injuries, but Svante and Malena put together all their emails and written evidence and took their case to the school board, which ultimately ruled in their favor. But Greta was still hated and bullied. She was misunderstood. She was different and being different was like a curse. The more they bullied her, the stronger she got.

The days in the library were memorable for Greta. Her teacher would come in, always on time, during recess and lunch and Greta would open her books and soak up every subject she was taught. Her photographic memory helped her to always score highly on every test and Greta not only learned a lot from her teacher, she learned a lot about people. At least one person. And herself.

Her eating improved and she graduated from pancakes stuffed with rice, to salmon and rice and avocados and as summer approached when she went for her next diagnostic interview at the Stockholm Center, the school psychologist showed up to give her support.

Although Greta did not gain any weight, she stopped losing it and never varied from her diet, no matter what. She also never ate in front of anyone else, which was attributed to her Asperger's.

The documentary about the garbage island still haunted her and even though no one ever mentioned it again, she couldn't get it out of her mind. She felt a connection to it. She studied the climate and learned all the terms. She knew that flying in an airplane contributed to her carbon footprint, which, when added to everyone else in the world, was one of the major causes of the climate crisis.

"If we all keep living the way we do now on planet Earth, we will need 4.2 Earths to survive!" she said over the dinner table. She had found something to believe in. To live for. It was leading her out of the darkness of depression and into the light of singleness of purpose. She actually felt happy again.

Her younger sister, Beata, however, became disgruntled and blamed Greta and grew worse, emotionally, claiming her mother and father favored Greta more than her. Svante decided to take Beata on a trip to Sardinia. By plane. Greta was invited but she vehemently refused to fly and stayed home. "Cutting down on flying is the best way for us to cut down our carbon footprint," she scolded.

After landing in Sardinia, her father and sister drove to their hotel near the Straight of Bonifacio, at the tip of the island. When Svante and Beata returned from their holiday in Sardinia, at the close of the summer, he gave up flying altogether.

Greta decided to dedicate her education to learning as much about the climate as possible. She couldn't shake the horrors of the garbage island and global crisis, so she embraced it. The old joke was that everyone was talking about the weather but no one was doing anything about it. Well, the joke was on them. Climate and weather were two different things. And most adults in the world didn't get it. Even the President of the United States believed the old wives' tales instead of the science. She sensed a door was opening for her and she was always taught that when a door opened, to go through it. She decided to do something about it.

Her weeks in the school library were not only spent reading important literature with her teacher, she dedicated half her time to studying climate science so she could understand how mankind could create an island of garbage as big as the country of Mexico. She would get up every hour to stretch and oftentimes go outside. She became so good at it, she was able to teach her teacher a thing or two about the climate.

In the winter, the smoke continued to belch from the chimneys in Stockholm and she saw them as streams of poison, greenhouse gases, rising on the winds and transforming the atmosphere. They were turning the land she loved into an invisible garbage dump. She was terrified they were turning the world into one big garbage island.

She thought about her father's great-grand-mother's cousin, Svante Arrhenius, and decided it was time to learn more about him, so she found a private place where no one could find her, nor see her read. She found one of his books on a musty library shelf and pulled it out and sat down against a shelf, partially lit by sunlight streaming in from an ancient nearby hand-cut glass paned window. As she read, the story of Svante Arrhenius unfolded before her imagination, and amazed her.

CHAPTER EIGHT

THE SIGN

S vante Arrhenius was obsessed with the different glaciations the planet had suffered over the millennia. Glaciations was another way of saying Ice Age. In 1896, he was the first person to predict that emissions of carbon dioxide from the burning of fossil fuels and other combustion processes were large enough to cause global warming. Now, in 2015, everyone was talking about global warming. But what were they really doing about it? Nothing. At least, that's how it seemed. For Greta, everyone should have been doing everything about it all the time. But there were still so many people in the world who denied this was even happening, including the President of the United States, who Greta's mom sincerely believed embodied the worst in modern society. But even if someone believed it was real—did they care what their governments were doing to fight it?

Greta slammed the thick volume shut and leaped to her feet. She charged across the marble floor to the main desk and deposited the book on it with a thud and continued on out of the building.

"Don't you want to check out the book?" the librarian shouted after her.

"I have a copy at home!" Greta replied and disappeared out the library door.

Twenty minutes later, Greta sat across from her mother and father at the dining table, the plate in front of her filled with slices of avocado, gnocchi, and silver-dollar sized pancakes.

"Calm down, Greta, you're getting all charged up," Malena said, reaching across the table to touch her daughter's hand.

Greta got up on her knees on the chair so she could lean across the table. "I am calm, but I don't know if you realize, there isn't much time! Burning stuff like heating oil and coal and fossil fuels are putting more and more carbon dioxide into our atmosphere! It's being trapped because there is too much of the stuff and that is causing Earth to heat up! We need to do something!"

"We are. We do what we can," her dad said. "As a family. We know we are facing a disaster but we don't have the power to do it all."

Greta slumped back in her chair. "That's the problem. It was left to the adults, and they aren't doing anything."

"You mean, they aren't doing enough," her father corrected her.

Greta drilled him with her eyes. "I meant exactly what I said, Father."

Malena looked at her husband. "She's right. Half the world doesn't even believe we have anything to do with it, let alone doing something about it."

Behind them, in the living room, the television blared news from the US state of Florida, where students at a High School called Parkland were speaking of going on strike. When Greta heard them talking, she couldn't resist and got up from the table.

She peered at the screen intently as the students' story unfolded. Malena also couldn't resist. She got up from the table and went over to Greta and watched with her. They didn't budge until the news story was over. "What if someone did that for the climate?" Malena said absently.

Greta's head jerked to her mother. She was right. "You just gave me an idea," she said.

"I did?" Malena said.

Greta nodded. "I think I know what I have to do."

"What's that?" Svante asked, spooning another red potato onto his plate. "What do you have to do?"

Greta stood up with a smile. "It's so obvious! Mom said it. I should have thought of it sooner! I have to go on strike!"

At that precise moment, the Prime Minister of Sweden came on television, speaking about climate change. "Sometimes, we humans cheat ourselves," he said. "For instance, it is humans who got us into it."

Greta leaped to her feet. "He's lying!" she screamed.

Malena gasped. "Greta, no! Of course, it was humans! Don't tell me you believe that we don't have nothing to do with it!"

Greta looked at her with saucer eyes and burst out laughing. "Of course not, Mom! It's just that what he said isn't true. I am human and I haven't done anything to make climate change worse! Beata either! You either! Or Dad!"

"He wasn't saying all humans did this," Malena said. "It was a general statement. He is saying it's nobody's fault, so no one is to blame."

Greta remained silent for a moment. "If that is what he meant, then he is lying. Because someone *is* to blame. This much greenhouse gas is not created naturally. A few hundred companies around the world are doing it. They are to blame for all the CO2 emissions. They are killing our planet. Aren't we going to do anything? Are we going to let them get away with it? To save the planet, we must fight them."

"What do you mean, fight?" Svante asked.

"Strike. Demonstrate, like the kids in Florida. Everywhere," Greta replied.

"Well, when you put it that way—" Malena said and let the sentence trail off.

Greta looked serious. She was on the verge of tears. "I did the math," she said. "They're saying that anything beyond 2050 will find it almost impossible to survive."

"Why are you worried about that?" Malena asked. "That's a long way off."

"I'll be forty-seven and my generation will be doomed."

Malena studied her daughter. She was correct.

"We have to save the planet."

"You're right, Greta, we do," Malena replied.

"In 2078 and 2080, Beata and I will celebrate our seventy-fifth birthday. I know what you're thinking—how do I know we'll live that long? Well, Grandfather is ninety-three. And his father passed away at ninety-nine. We will live that long and we will most likely have children and grandchildren and what kind of a world will we leave them?"

"Well," Malena said, flustered. "Why are you worried about that?"

"Why are you not worried?" Greta replied.

Malena bit her lip, then said, "What does your strike look like? What do you need?"

"A sign. It has to be a big sign," Greta said, growing more and more excited thinking about it. "Like the kinds of posters I make for my science projects in class. With big lettering that says **SCHOOL STRIKE FOR CLIMATE**. White with big black lettering so everybody gets the message."

Greta looked to her father and waited for him to respond, but he just stared back without saying a word for what seemed like an eternity. "Well? You haven't said a peep about our future, what do you think about a sign?"

"If it rains, a paper poster will get soaked and it will turn to mush," he said.

"There is a large piece of leftover plywood on the side of the house," Greta said. "Can we use that?"

"Good call. Your sign should be made of wood," Svante said.

"And paint it white," Greta said. "It will be like a shield!"

Svante flashed a broad smile and Greta hugged him. "Exactly."

The sign became their project. They went to the hardware store to buy the white paint for the background and black paint for the lettering. They brought everything home to work on it. On the way back, they passed a toy store with plastic dinosaurs in the window. They stopped to look. "Too bad they disappeared. Life would definitely not be boring with them around."

"They'd eat us," Greta said and Svante chuckled.

"Do you know why the dinosaurs disappeared?"

"The major theory is that an asteroid hit the Yucatan Peninsula," Greta replied. "An asteroid is a giant meteorite."

"I know what it is," Svante said.

"But there is more to it than that."

"Oh?"

"What we have now is unlimited growth on a limited planet," she said with a sad look. "There have been five mass extinctions in our history."

Svante studied her. "We're not talking about dinosaurs anymore, are we?"

"I read that German researchers discovered that seventy-five percent of the insect species on Earth have gone extinct."

The thought unnerved him. "That many?"

Greta nodded. "And the bird population in France has collapsed."

"What does that mean?"

"I'm not sure," Greta replied. "Have you ever heard of Kevin Anderson?"

Svante took Greta's hand in his and they continued walking. "Yes. he's a climate science professor, in Manchester, England."

"He said, the main problem with humans is that we always do everything all at once at high speed."

"That sounds about right. But what does that have to do with the price of tea in China?"

"I don't get it. It doesn't have anything to do with tea or China."

"It's an expression. A joke."

"Oh, I get it. You're talking about randomness," Greta giggled. "Anyway, Kevin Anderson said 'Humankind is like a meteorite with consciousness, but without a conscience.' Do you know what he meant?"

Now it was Svante's turn to laugh. "Consider the dinosaurs," he said. "Destroyed by a giant meteorite."

"Right," Greta said.

"Now consider man as a meteorite."

Greta thought about it. "Oh my God," she said. "He's saying we're about to do it again!"

Svante grinned. "Only this time without a giant rock."

Greta giggled.

Svante opened the gate to their home and held it for his daughter. She stopped in front of him before going in. "Dad?"

"Yes?"

"I think what Kevin Anderson said is a sign."

CHAPTER NINE

MOM

As Greta and Svante worked on her *School Strike for Climate* sign, Malena walked Beata to dance school, which was a mile from their home. Even though it was only a mile, it took them an hour because of Beata's emotional limitations. Like her sister, she was also diagnosed with a mild case of Asperger's as well as something called OCD, which was an abbreviation for obsessive-compulsive disorder. In other words, her mind had many constraints on her. For instance, on the way to dance school, Beata could not walk on certain squares in the sidewalk and street and she always had to put her left foot first. This was the compulsive part of obsessive-compulsive. Whenever she made a mistake, she had to start over. It was exhausting raising two girls with these constraints, but Malena was sympathetic to them, remembering having similar limitations when she was a little girl and although she drove her own mother crazy, she knew it was not Greta's or Beata's fault.

When they arrived at the dance studio, Malena sat outside the class so Beata could see her through a crack in the door while she took the class. She didn't move from her post until the class was over. She knew if Beata could not see her through the crack in the door, she might panic.

A motorbike went by and as its rider shifted gears, Malena knew each progressive gear was in G, then F, then D, then E. When the motorbike was gone, she could hear the birds again, which were a different story. The F9 chord was a part of all of them. Every noise in Malena's life had a connected musical note. It was why she became a singer. It was also why she was patient with her daughters when, among other things, they suffered from misophonia, an extreme sensitivity to noise; although when they complained growing up, they had no problem making their own noises.

Malena looked up and saw the dance class was letting out. It was time for the long left-footed walk home.

Back at home, Greta and her father finished the strike sign. She thought it was a thing of beauty. She also thought that thought was illogical. There's nothing beautiful about going on strike for climate change. Greta felt all their lives depended on it. Not only was climate change not beautiful, neither were its symbols. Like her sign.

When Malena and Beata returned from dance school, Malena made Greta her lunch. Greta always ate the same thing so it wasn't a surprise: two pancakes with rice, warmed up in the microwave, without topping or sauce. No jam, no butter. Just pure pancakes and pure rice. It had to smell exactly right or she couldn't eat it.

For dinner, Greta only ate pasta, two potatoes, and an avocado. No more, no less. Satisfied her sign was complete, Greta went with her mother to the market. As they shopped, Greta went off to find an item on their list and came across a table filled with waffles and cream, laid out for anyone to purchase and eat. Ten plates, ten mini-waffles. Greta bent down and sniffed them all and the woman running the table was taken aback by her actions.

"Now you have to eat them and pay for them," the woman said.

Greta just stared at her. She wasn't one of the family so there was no need to speak.

Malena saw the incident and rushed over. "I'm so sorry, she has Asperger's," she said.

"I don't know what that is, but why won't she say anything? I told her she sniffed all of them and came too close to them so I can't sell them so they are hers now." She talked fast and Greta thought she sounded upset.

Malena contained herself. "She has selective mutism. I'm sorry for your troubles, it won't happen again."

"I'm sure it won't, but I'm afraid she might have touched them with the tip of her nose or worse, breathed on them, so you'll have to buy them all."

"But they're on—open plates. How will we carry them?"

"You don't have to carry them; you just have to eat them." She shrugged. "Or toss them."

"No!" Greta screamed and everyone looked.

Malena managed a smile and spoke softly: "All of them?"

"Well, she breathed on all of them."

Malena looked at the plates. Ten of them. Looked to Greta. "Stop smelling," she said to her, then returned her attention to the lady. She wasn't going to budge. Finally, Malena shrugged, threw down some money, grabbed a fork, and started eating.

Greta watched with keen interest.

It took a while, but Malena finally finished all the waffles and cream.

They left the market pushing their cart full of the food they bought but Malena moved a little slower than normal because she was so full. "Mom?" Greta asked as they crossed the parking lot.

"Yes?" Malena replied. "Don't tell me, you're ready to apologize?"

Greta looked at her funny. "No, I was just wondering when I would be allowed to smell again."

When Malena discussed flying with Greta, she stressed the importance of her getting around Europe even though she was retired from her career, but Greta was prepared for the argument. "If we stop flying," Greta always said, "then someone will have to invent something that doesn't destroy our planet that we can use to move from one place to another. But it will never happen if we don't put our foot down."

She said a lot more, a lot of scary stuff, Malena thought. But that was the gist of it. She was an inspiration to her mother and Malena quit flying for good.

Greta's argument for the climate was terrifying and convincing. Planes flew on fuel, fuel polluted the atmosphere, the atmosphere was killing the planet. Greta was moved by her mother's gesture, but it was too logical a decision to go overboard with any kind of effusive emotional reaction. Let's just say,

Greta was relieved another human being on planet Earth had come to their senses in time.

Malena, on the other hand, came to believe in her decision wholeheartedly and stopped blaming Greta, and at the end of the very warm Swedish summer of 2018, around the same time that Greta decided to go on strike, Malena gave up flying. And at the same time, Svante gave up shopping for things he did not need. He also gave up meat. Everybody in the Thunberg household was getting on the same page.

"If the richest ten percent of the world population would adjust their emission levels to the EU average, it would reduce world output by thirty percent!" Kevin Anderson said on television. "Rapid measures. That is what we need. With these, we could really do something. We could buy some time."

CHAPTER TEN

SUPERPOWERS

The ride to the Parliament building that August was already hot by 8 am in the morning. The sun had been up for almost four hours and it seemed as if everyone in Stockholm was out on the streets. Greta held the painted *strike for climate* sign under her arm and steered her bicycle with the other. A lot of pedestrians looked, but no one had time to engage. When she arrived at the Parliament steps, she leaned her sign against the aging bricks and addressed the people who streamed back and forth in both directions, hurrying to their jobs. Students laughed as they passed her on their way to class.

"Much of the world's population does not have the slightest idea what climate change means to us," she bellowed out to anyone who would listen. Not many did, although plenty of them giggled and chuckled.

"Does your mommy know where you are?" one boy said as he sailed past on his bicycle.

"Get to school!" another woman shouted at her.

A group of students stopped and applauded her.

Greta blushed. She realized everything she had done so far, was worth it.

She took in a lungful of Stockholm morning air, then plunked down next to her sign and waited in silence.

On the second day, a man with meaty hands and athletic calves, wearing sporting clothes, came over to her and handed her a large bar of Swiss chocolate. "We love what you are doing! Never give up," he said and moved on.

Greta put the chocolate bar down beside her in the shade of her sign. It was not on her Asperger's menu, but the thought moved her.

The reporters showed up after lunch and spent the rest of the afternoon with her and went away happy with a story they could file.

On the third day, she brought a small stack of flyers explaining how humans were dooming the planet and that the adults did not seem to be bothered with any of it, because at least in Sweden, there certainly was no real commitment to change. The wording was hers and it was harsh. "We kids often don't do what you tell us to do," she wrote. She was speaking of the failure of the adults to protect the planet for her generation. "And since you grown-ups don't give a shit about my future, I won't either."

"There is a vote coming on September 9," she said to anyone who would listen. It was very brave of her because she had never spoken to anyone outside of her immediate family in a long, long time. "We want awareness of climate policy to be on the ballot."

By the end of the fifth day, all the flyers were gone and she was getting used to speaking. It wasn't so bad. No problem is as bad as my solution to it, she thought and chuckled to herself. She sensed that something was finally working. People listened and she didn't fear talking to strangers anymore.

And then one day, a couple people came and asked if they could join in.

From that moment on, she was never alone again.

By the tenth day, there were twenty citizens sitting with her in protest, striking together for the climate. They believed in Greta just as much as Greta believed in what she was doing. Greta shared the chocolate she had saved but did not try any of it herself. It was not for her. Pancakes and rice. Now you're talking.

A few days before election day, Karin Bäckstrand showed up at her favorite place to sit during the strike. Bäckstrand was a climate-policy researcher at Stockholm University, which meant to Greta that she should know what she was talking about.

She kneeled down to speak to Greta. "I hear you're staying here until the vote," she said.

"Two days before the vote," Greta said. "That's my plan."

"What are you expecting to happen?" the woman asked.

"Do you mean what am I hoping for?" Greta countered.

"Sure," the woman replied.

Greta riveted her with a gaze. "Actually, someone—a Member of Parliament—told me there was nothing on the agenda about climate change," she said. "So, whatever it is I am thinking, it's not unrealistic."

The woman was surprised at Greta's knowledge and vocabulary. "Yes, it was to be expected. What need do we have? Everyone in Sweden already agrees we need to go fossil fuel free."

"And yet," Greta said, frowning. "We are failing."

"Is that why you are here, Greta?" Bäckstrand asked.

Greta opened what was left of the chocolate bar and offered it to the woman. "Chocolate?"

"No, thank you," the woman said.

"It was a gift from someone who worried about me. I was always taught to not waste food."

"Oh, very well," the woman said and took the rest of the chocolate and Greta grinned broadly, happy she had not wasted it. "How old are you?" the woman asked.

"Fifteen," she said.

"Well, what are you worried about?"

"I'm worried that when I am halfway through my life, that there will be no world to live in. Nothing we are doing foresees a future past 2050. That's what I'm worried about. What happens next? What then?"

The woman blushed. "I don't think you need to worry. We in Sweden are in the middle of an economic boom. That's what is then," she said. "But in the meantime, keep doing what you're doing." Embarrassed, the woman walked away.

"I will," Greta said to herself.

She sat on the warm cobblestones for three weeks, striking for the climate, every day of the week. At the end or her last day in front of Parliament, two days before the vote, she packed up her sign, climbed on her bicycle, and headed home. She had more than one hundred followers and they waved goodbye to her and each went their own separate way to branch out and become part of a much larger climate change movement. Greta had become a fixture on the cobblestones of Sweden's parliament.

She knew she had to have a new plan. Not only did she not want to stay out of school forever, she wanted to return. Her new plan had to include that. She trusted her instincts as she grew stronger. Although she never ate any of the food offered to her during her five-day-a-week climate strike, she began to experiment at home with new things. Her mother caught her eating a falafel one night. "I thought you only ate pancakes and rice!" she said.

Greta smiled slightly "So did I, Mom, she said. "Maybe I'm recovering."

Malena smiled. Something good was happening to her daughter.

"I know I'm not like everyone else," Greta said. "People think I'm weird but I don't care."

"You are special," Malena said.

"I know I have limitations," Greta said, "But you always tell me these limitations are my superpowers."

CHAPTER ELEVEN

FRIDAYS FOR FUTURE & BEYOND

After three weeks of striking for the climate, on the Friday night before her final weekend, Greta and her mother and father and Beata sat around the kitchen table and worked on Greta's speech that she was going to give the following morning, a Saturday. She was terrified until Moses waddled into the room and laid down under the table and rested his nose on her foot. Roxy, their newly-adopted dog was there too. It was a fun night. They ate silver dollar-sized pancakes and Greta was so excited she was jumping out of her skin.

The next morning, the day after her last day of her original school strike, September 8, the day before the Sunday vote, Greta gave her first speech on the steps of the Parliament building in Stockholm. This speech ultimately became a speech entitled *Our Lives Are in Your Hands*, in what was to be her first climate march. She stood on the steps and her knees shook. Over one hundred people stood nearby waiting for her to speak. It seemed like only a week ago that she could not speak to anyone other than her family and now she was about to talk to an especially large, imposing crowd of complete strangers.

"Last summer, climate scientist Johan Rockström and some other people wrote that we have at most three years to reverse growth in greenhouse-gas emissions if we're going to reach the goals set in the Paris Agreement."

As she spoke, she grew more and more relaxed. "In Sweden, we live our lives as if we had the resources of 4.2 planets. Our carbon footprint is one of the ten worst in the world. This means that Sweden steals 3.2 years of natural resources from future generations every year. Those of us who are part of these future generations would like Sweden to stop doing that. Right now."

The audience chuckled, but they were uncomfortable. Everyone was responsible and everyone knew Greta spoke the truth.

"A lot of people say that Sweden is a small country, that it doesn't matter what we do. But I think that if a few girls can get headlines all over the world just by not going to school for a few weeks, imagine what we could do together if we wanted to."

Greta ended her brief talk by saying, "So please, treat the climate crisis like the acute crisis it is and give us a future. Our lives are in your hands." She looked up and shielded her eyes from the sun. "Join me," she said.

Her fellow students who stood around listening just shook their heads and moved on.

"I'll join you," one man said. Then another. Then two women, and before the hour was out, she was surrounded by over one hundred people, mostly young.

The next school day, Greta's class piled into an electric school bus and went on a field trip to the local museum. Greta liked the sound her feet made when they walked on the large slabs of marble on the floor. They echoed and betrayed the hollowness of the hall. She wished her mom was there to tell which keys her feet were in, they seemed to be playing two different notes.

She made a beeline for the new exhibit on climate change and entered the separate hall carefully. It took less than a minute for her to discover the statistics included in the exhibit on the carbon footprint of meat production was all wrong. As she wandered slowly, growing more and more unhappy, she found many more things factually wrong. Eventually, she could not endure it anymore and she spun around and marched out and found a place to sit near the exit to the museum and stayed there until the field trip was over.

The teacher came over to ask her what was wrong but she refused to speak. She could talk all right but, in that moment, there was nothing to talk about. She knew the only thing that would change what she didn't like was to act. Seeing an exhibit of misinformation about her favorite subject infuriated her. Not only did she see all the mistakes in the museum, she clearly saw her next plan before her. She was driven and inspired.

That evening at supper, Greta ate carefully but ravenously. Her exercise walking around the museum had made her hungry. Beata ate quietly for once and Malena was burning to talk. She cleared her throat. "I suppose you already know the election resulted in nothing," she said.

Greta looked up from her meal and nodded. "It was ineffectual," she replied. "But at this point, I don't think it matters. The issue of climate crisis is not going to collapse because some political party got the most votes."

"Yes," Svante chimed in. "But it's politics that is needed to prevent climate change."

Greta shook her head. "You mean a climate catastrophe. There is nothing that can prevent climate change, we can only prevent climate change from destroying us. Unfortunately, the politics that are needed to prevent a climate catastrophe don't exist," she said and spooned some avocado. "So, we need to change the system. We need to do all things. We need to act as if we are already in a crisis. Like there's a war going on. That's what Kevin Anderson says and so, that's what I say."

"You keep talking like that, did you know some people are already saying you're mad?" Malena asked with a grin. "You better watch out or they're going to try to cure you."

Greta giggled. "Aspie kids aren't mad, Mom, you know that," she said. "And there *is* no cure. Hey, you know what I heard. I heard that madness doesn't *need* to be cured, it needs to be liberated."

They all shared a laugh. Even Beata.

"How do you plan to do that?" Svante asked, dreading her reply. "More signs?"

"No. I'm going to go on strike."

"You already did that."

"Let's call it Strike 2.0 or something. This time, on Fridays only. Every Friday. As of right now there are many of us, not many students, not many politicians, but plenty of real people. They feel just as we all do, that without doing something we have no future. So, my Friday strike will be called *Fridays For Future*." She watched as her father spooned some more noodles onto his plate. "May I have some of those noodles?"

Malena shot a look to her husband and Svante shrugged and served a ladle-full of noodles onto her plate. Greta immediately began eating them.

Malena watched for a while, then: "I didn't know you liked noodles," she said with caution.

"They looked good," Greta nodded. "Did I mention I like falafel too?"

Malena gave her husband another look, then relaxed. "Okay, so we've got some changes going on here. But what about school, Greta? What are you going to do about school?"

"I'll go to school four days a week and on Friday, I'll sit outside Parliament with my sign. My teacher has already agreed to catch me up on my what I miss on *Fridays For Future* days. Besides, people are always in a good mood on Friday," she said with a smile, then continued to eat.

After the Parliament held its vote on the following day, Sunday, September 9, and failed to even mention climate change in its policies, Greta created a new plan for her life that included going to school and striking. She called it *Fridays For Future* and she returned to the cobblestones a second time, the following Friday. She traveled by bicycle and she sat alongside her hand-painted sign all day. She was quickly becoming famous and many hundreds of people walked by in both directions in front of the Parliament building, just to get a look at the girl who was striking for the climate.

Around Europe, many school strikes had sprung up in that week and they were all modeled after Greta's concept of a school strike for the climate. Her name and picture began showing up in all the newspapers, first buried deep in the news section and gradually making its way to the front page.

And as all good news stories go, the longer Greta made her presence known outside of Parliament, the more the word of her movement spread. It spread across Europe. It spread across the United Kingdom. And finally, it spread around the world.

That night, Greta couldn't sleep and Malena noticed and came in and sat on the side of her bed and held her hand. "What's wrong, Greta?" she asked.

"I'm scared," she said.

"Why?" Malena said. "Are you afraid your strike isn't going to work?"

"No," Greta said. "I'm scared because it *is* working. There were people who came from all over Europe to see me."

"But that's wonderful!" Malena said.

"But what if I mess up?"

Malena smiled and hugged her oldest daughter. "Are you doing the right thing?" she asked and Greta nodded. "Then you can't mess this up."

Greta went to school all that week and on Friday showed up in the usual place again. She continued to demand a future for herself and her generation. She cried, and the press came to her. "Why are you still here?" one reporter from the *New Scientist* magazine asked her.

"Because I am a massive reserve of stubbornness!" she exclaimed and they shared a laugh. She wondered aloud why it was working. "The idea was to sit outside the Swedish Parliament for three weeks. I think the timing and the concept must have been right," she continued.

The following month, in October, Malena rushed into Greta's room and woke her up. "Greta, wake up!"

Greta sat straight up; eyes wide, terrified. "What is it?!"

Malena was waving a letter around. "You have been invited to London for the Extinction Rebellion!"

Greta wiped the sleep out of her eyes. "We'll drive."

Malena looked at her daughter and shook her head in amazement. "Do you want to think about it?"

Greta grinned. "I just did."

The Thunbergs drove to London in their electric car. It took twenty hours, partly on the E4, among other highways, once more with zero emissions. The most fun was the Chunnel between France and England. Oxford Circus in Central London was amassed with people lying in the street. London took climate change seriously and were grateful to have Greta's support and help.

Later, in Parliament Square, Greta gave another speech, this one entitled *Almost Everything is Black and White*. It was called by the media a *Declaration of Rebellion, an Extinction Rebellion*. As usual, it was a family affair and for Greta it had to be about her generation's future, a future that was obviously no longer guaranteed, despite what the grown-ups were saying. It terrified her and gave her nightmares and she translated that into action.

"When you think about the future today, you don't think beyond the year 2050. By then, I will, in the best case, not even have lived half my life. What happens next? In the year 2078, I will celebrate my seventy-fifth birthday. What we do or don't do, right now, will affect my entire life, and the lives of my children and grandchildren. When school started in August this year, I decided that this was enough. I sat myself down on the ground outside the Swedish Parliament."

Everyone always got around to asking about her father's great-grandmother's cousin, Svante Arrhenius, who knew all of this ages ago and learned a lot from the founder of climate science, John Tyndall. Each in their own generation, they warned the world. Now it was the 21st century, and things were much, much worse on planet Earth. And now, it was looking as if it was Greta's turn to do the warning.

"Some people say that I should study to become a climate scientist so that I can *solve the climate crisis*. But the climate crisis has already been solved. We already have all the facts and solutions. All we have to do is to wake up and change."

After the Extinction Rebellion, the Thunbergs turned their electric car around and headed home to Stockholm.

Malena turned around in the front seat of the car and watched her daughters sleep in the back. Beata rested her head on her older sister's shoulder. Greta sensed someone was watching and opened an eye and saw her mother smiling.

"Still frightened?" Malena asked softly, not wanting to wake up Beata.

Greta shook her head. "We have too much to do."

CHAPTER TWELVE

UNSTOPPABLE

In Stockholm, the crowds grew while Greta received letters from all around the world about school strikes by children who believed in Greta, children just like her. Greta looked out over the crowds that gathered wherever she went. "This is another sign," she told her father.

It started to rain. "So is this," he said and they giggled and took shelter. It rained all November in Stockholm and Greta repainted her sign to withstand the colder elements of the Swedish weather while she stood vigil outside the Parliament, holding to her commitment.

In December, Greta piled into the family electric car with the rest of the family again and this time drove to Poland. It took two days, stopping along the way to sleep, again, with zero emissions. She was nervous when she addressed the 24th annual Conference of the Parties to the United Nations Framework Convention on Climate Change, also known as COP24, in Katowice, and saying her speech out loud for thousands made her cry. Her speech was from the heart and brutally honest, her message to the world had evolved. "In the year 2078, I will celebrate my seventy-fifth birthday. If I have children, then maybe they will spend that day with me. Maybe they will ask about you. Maybe they will ask why you didn't do anything, while there was still time to act. You say that you love your children above everything else. And yet you are stealing from their future."

Greta's appearance at COP24 was devastating to those in attendance and she was immediately invited to the Davos Economic Forum in Switzerland in January 2019.

Greta and her father folded up the four-season tent. "Sixteen," she said, holding up the tent stakes.

"Yes, sixteen tent stakes, that's all of them," Svante said and took them from her and put them in their pouch and folded them into the tent and packed it into their car.

"No, silly, I'm sixteen," Greta said.

Svante cocked his head like Moses and smiled. "So you are! Perhaps it is another one of your signs," he said with a grin.

Greta stifled a laugh. "Doubtful."

While many delegates flew to Davos in private jets, Greta and her father took a 32-hour train ride from Stockholm.

Many of the delegates stayed in luxury hotels, but Greta and her father camped-out in a tent in zero-degrees weather.

They slept in sleeping bags. On the ground.

"Ugh," Svante muttered in the dark.

"The smells are amazing," he heard Greta say, somewhere else in the tent.

"I'm glad you like them," he answered.

"I like sleeping on the ground," Greta said.

"Not me," Svante said.

It was silent for a while. Svante stayed awake until he heard Greta breathe heavily, then snore lightly. Then he closed his eyes and went to sleep.

On a Thursday of that week, Greta gave an impromptu speech at a luncheon where a number of superstars from around the world attended, like Bono from the band U2, will.i.am from The Black Eyed Peas, Salesforce CEO Marc Benioff, and former Goldman Sachs President Gary Cohn. She gave them no mercy. Her message was that despite the snow and ice on the ground, the world was on fire.

"Some people say that the climate crisis is something that we have created, but that is not true," she said to the Davos Conference audience. "Because if everyone is guilty, then no one is to blame. And someone *is* to blame!"

Her speech was met with silence for what seemed like an eternity. Then Bono stood up and started clapping, louder and louder, and one-by-one the attendees joined in, which led to a standing ovation. Bono shouted "Bravo!"

Greta had arrived on the world stage and when she returned to the cobblestones in front of the Stockholm Parliament building, in March 2019, she was now a figurehead for a worldwide movement and the cobblestones had become an iconic place for climate protests. Elsewhere, there were over 700 protests going on in 71 countries around the world.

That night, back in her own bed, Greta stared at the ceiling until her mother noticed and came in from the living room where they were watching television.

"What are you doing?" Malena asked.

"Staring at the ceiling," Greta replied.

"What do you see?"

Greta grinned. "A very boring ceiling."

"Can't sleep?" she asked, laying down next to her.

Greta got up on one elbow to face her mother. "If there were seven-hundred protests going on all around the world, all based on your idea, would *you* be able to sleep?"

Malena chuckled. "Don't forget that is seven-hundred protests in seventy-one countries."

Greta groaned. "Great. You just made it worse."

Mother and daughter shared a laugh. "Stay with me," Greta whispered.

"All right," Malena said.

In the following weeks, while Greta returned to her perch in front of Parliament in Stockholm, elsewhere, three deputies of the Norwegian Parliament nominated her for a Nobel Peace Prize.

By then, Greta had already created various social media accounts. Her favorite was her Twitter account. It was fast. It was like writing headlines for newspapers, and she had over a million followers, almost overnight. She made the announcement about the Nobel nomination on her Twitter account first. "I am honored and very grateful for this nomination," she said to her followers, then returned to her strike, making sure everyone could see her hand-painted sign.

In April, she addressed the European Parliament. The following day, she traveled to Vatican City in Rome for a general audience with Pope Francis. She stood behind a short barrier with her father and a translator who knew Pope Francis, and had a very good glimpse of the Pope. He was a great proponent of climate change and she was a fan. But when he started walking her way, she almost had a panic attack. And when he stopped to speak with their translator, she lost her voice.

"Your holiness, this is Greta Thunberg, the climate change advocate who is well-known all around the world," their translator said in English and the Pope did something amazing. He took Greta's hand. And she instantly relaxed.

"Congratulations," he said.

"Thank you," Greta said. "Thank you for standing up for the climate and speaking the truth."

He smiled wisely, she thought, then said, "Continue to work. Continue to work." Then he was gone.

Svante studied his daughter as the crowd around them dispersed. "How was that?" he asked.

"I'm so happy we came. I'm so happy I was able to make climate change a motivating force, instead of a source of paralyzing depression."

Svante looked relieved. He and Malena had gone through a lot. "Sötnos, me too," he said, calling her sweet nose.

Suddenly, a microphone was shoved in her face. It was a local newswoman. "Greta, you yourself are considered a beacon of hope. What was it like speaking to another beacon—the Pope?" the woman asked, her recorder rolling.

"Amazing," Greta replied.

"Where do you find the energy to do what you do?"

Greta nodded. She had heard this question before. "Well, I'm young, that helps. It takes a lot of energy and I don't have much spare time. But I keep reminding myself why I am doing this, and then I just try to do as much as I can," she said.

"What about school?"

"Oh, I keep up with my homework. I'm in the top five in my class, at least that's what my father says." They all shared a laugh.

When the newswoman left, Greta looked at her hand. The hand touched by the Pope. "He had rough hands," she said to her father. "Workers hands. Are my hands rough?"

Svante felt her hands. "They're getting there.

Greta smiled to herself. Continuing to work was not a problem for her, a girl with Asperger's, with a sole mission in life. Of course, now, she was not only a massive reserve of stubbornness, she was hungry.

In May, Greta appeared on the cover of *Time Magazine* and was featured on the television show *60 Minutes* in Australia. It was around that time on her busy schedule that she was invited to participate at the United Nations climate talks in September. In the United States. That meant somehow getting there without flying. That challenge became a reality soon thereafter. She would sail across the North Atlantic to the United States aboard the *Malizia II*, the most beautiful solar-powered open-cockpit mono-hull racing yacht in the world.

CHAPTER THIRTEEN

THERE ARE SIGNS EVERYWHERE

Greta stood on the pitching deck of the zero-emissions racing yacht, *Malizia II*, and took questions from the press before sailing away for the United States. "You have been characterized as an *ignorant teenage climate puppet* by Steve Milloy, a member of Donald Trump's transition team," the reporter said. "Do these kinds of attacks deter you in any way?"

"I welcome them," Greta replied.

Svante watched from a short distance away. His daughter looked defiant and as strong as anyone he'd ever known. He knew now that she had accepted who she was. He also knew that one minute they shared a tent in zero-degrees weather in Switzerland and now they were on the deck of a racing boat about to sail across the North Atlantic.

The Swedish press said it best. "Greta seems incapable of the cognitive dissonance that allows other people to lament what is happening to the climate one minute, then eat a steak, buy a car, or fly off for a weekend of fun the next. Although she believes political action far outweighs individual changes to consumer habits, she lives her values. She is a vegan, and only travels abroad by train."

Or electric car, Svante thought, although this time they had traveled by train.

Nearby, Greta faced the reporter who asked for her opinion of the name one of Trump's team had called her. "If they are attacking me, then that means they have no argument to speak of and their debate only involves attacking me. That means we've already won. We have become the bad guys who have to tell people these uncomfortable things because no one else wants to, or dares to."

Satisfied, the reporter stepped back. Then someone else in the gaggle shouted: "Go to school!"

She chuckled. "I'm taking the year off. Besides, why should we go to school when you won't listen to the educated?" Greta shouted back.

Skipper Boris Herrmann and the head of the *Malizia II* racing team, Pierre Casiraghi, a member of the Monaco royal family, ran up the German flag. The French-built *Malizia II* was made in Monaco and displayed the royal crest on her mainsail but registered in Hamburg, Germany, and so, sailed under German colors. Swedish documentary filmmaker Nathan Grossman was already on deck filming as Herrmann cast off the lines and pushed off.

A few minutes later, when the rain stopped at 3 pm, the *Malizia II* set sail from Plymouth, England, for New York Harbor with Greta and her father aboard. The sleek hydrofoil 60-foot gray single-hulled racing yacht with *Global Climate Action* painted on the bow along with the words *United Nations Climate Change*, would take two weeks at a brisk 25 knots per hour. Electricity was provided by solar panels. Greta waved from the deck, holding on tightly to the one of the furled sails up front. She was dressed in a dark water-resistant outfit, jacket and pants, with *Unite Behind the Science* stenciled on the chest. *Unite Behind the Science* was also printed along the yardarms of the boat along with the Greta hashtag #FridaysForFuture.

They were on a southerly route to avoid the headwinds, always looking for the softer way: softer meaning calm winds and smooth sailing as opposed to blowing wind and pouring rain.

The conditions were spartan, which meant there were not only no luxuries, there wasn't even a toilet. There were, however, buckets, in back, in the stern. Blue buckets with white writing.

There was no room for shyness on this voyage.

There was plenty of electricity, however. The solar panels were installed across the center of the deck so you could walk on them and another set that ran along each side of the hull. In case of bad weather, the boat was equipped with a way to gather energy through the water flow as it cut through the ocean.

Greta had no time to get seasick. The rough seas sailing out of Plymouth were the perfect ice-breaker for what was to come on the North Atlantic. Greta brought her pack down to her sleeping quarters and took inventory of what she had brought along: a bunch of books and eight writing journals and a whole slew of freeze-dried vegan food, the kinds of meals you bring on backpacking treks.

When she returned above deck, the skipper, Boris, showed her how to use the satellite phone. It not only could be used to place voice calls and emergency calls if needed; it could also be used as a hotspot to connect to a satellite and the internet so Greta could keep up with her Twitter and other social media accounts and send texts and pictures to friends and family.

Later that night, Greta wrote her schedule as far as she knew it in one of the journals she brought along. She figured 14 days at sea minimum and then a number of weeks to organize protests in New York and around the world. She was scheduled to attend the United Nations climate summit in September, speaking at a youth summit on the 21st and then at the main meeting on September 23. The world leaders had all agreed, under the Paris Agreement, to keep global temperatures from rising to levels that would produce climate catastrophes. America did not, of course, as President Trump opted out of the Paris Agreement, citing that climate change was a hoax. Despite the agreement, between the other leaders of the democracies around the world, global emissions would continue to grow, Greta thought. None are really on track to meet their goals, but this would give them a chance to show that at least they'd been listening.

After that, she would spend the next nine months in the Americas. She wanted to go to Montreal, Canada, and later, in December, she planned on traveling again, this time to Chile, for the next round of United Nations-sponsored climate talks.

The next two weeks went by without incident. Greta continued to post to her Twitter and Instagram accounts and grew accustomed to the dehydrated backpacking meals she had packed.

Fourteen days later, off the coast of Canada, Boris made the decision to lower all sails and to ride out the rough seas off Nova Scotia. When the winds and rain calmed down, Boris gave the greenlight to make their way down the coast to New York. Still connected to the internet,

Greta tweeted a video of the rough seas and choppy waters as the yacht approached the United States.

Before bedding down for the night, Greta tweeted one last image of the voyage of her in their living quarters, the night before they hit New York.

All in all, fifteen days and many, many blue buckets later, Greta and her father were awakened by Boris in the early hours of the morning. They were off the coast of New York and in an hour or two they would sail straight into the marina at New York Harbor. Greta rushed up on deck, but Svante took his time. He stretched out on the bed one last time and decided it was definitely better than sleeping on the ground. In fact, he had enjoyed his sleep-filled nights onboard the *Malizia II* with no worries, other than survival at sea and, of course, the survival of planet Earth. He chuckled to himself and went up.

"Incredible," Greta muttered as she stared off into the darkness and saw the lights of the shoreline of New York. Her heart raced. She knew it wouldn't be long and they would be sailing into New York Harbor and staring at the busiest city in the world.

As the sun came up, the marina was calm and enveloped in fog, making it look very mysterious to Greta. There were many boats on the water and men and women on jet skis already out in the pre-dawn hours. Then she saw a sign. A sign as important as the sign Kevin Anderson saw when he likened man to a meteorite with consciousness, just as that giant asteroid that slammed into the Yucatan Peninsula during the Cretaceous and created a nuclear winter that helped end the reign of dinosaurs on the planet. And now humankind was doing it again, this time without any outside forces, just stubbornness and unwillingness to believe the educated, she thought.

She stared long and hard at the Statue of Liberty as they passed her. The ultimate symbol of freedom. She hoped she would once again welcome travelers to her shores someday.

As they sailed silently through the fog, she knew what she had to do when she stepped on dry land.

Her father stood beside her on the deck and draped a comforting arm around her. Minutes later, they dropped anchor.

Greta knew she would be organizing a strike once she settled on dry land. There would be protests for the climate and perhaps even against it, but those who fought for the planet organize here and everywhere around the world. There would be hundreds of them.

She leaned over the gunwale and dipped her hand in the water. It was warm. A motor boat pulled alongside to clear them through customs.

As they waited for customs and prepared to debark from their home for the past two weeks, other boats came to greet them, mostly with cameras rolling. The sea was as smooth as glass and warmer than usual. That was why she was here. Because it was too warm.

Finally, Greta would go to the UN and stand before the leaders of the world. Included among them would be some of the worst polluters in history. She hoped they would listen to what she had to say. And then do something about it. Earth was on fire and desperately needed saving. *The UN*, she thought. *That would be the perfect place for our first strike in New York.*

She smiled. It was time to get to work. She was excited and hopeful, a motivating force that had replaced her paralyzing depression.

All of that was gone now. She had finally found meaning, in a world that seemed meaningless to so many.

ABOUT THE AUTHOR

Michael Part was born in Sheboygan, Wisconsin and lives in the San Fernando Valley in Southern California with his wife and 5 children, 8 cats, and 1 parrot. He has been writing professionally since he was eighteen. His bestselling books are translated to 17 languages. He has written a number of motion pictures and television shows including the Disney classic, *A Kid in King Arthur's Court* and the groundbreaking anime feature, *Starbirds*!